GREAT PREDATORS

TARANTULA

by Ruth Strother

Content Consultant
Jason E. Bond
Professor and Director
Auburn University Museum of Natural History

CORE
LIBRARY

Published by ABDO Publishing Company, PO Box 398166, Minneapolis, MN 55439. Copyright © 2014 by Abdo Consulting Group, Inc. International copyrights reserved in all countries. No part of this book may be reproduced in any form without written permission from the publisher. The Core Library™ is a trademark and logo of ABDO Publishing Company.

Printed in the United States of America, North Mankato, Minnesota
052013
092013
 THIS BOOK CONTAINS AT LEAST 10% RECYCLED MATERIALS.

Editor: Lauren Coss
Series Designer: Becky Daum

Library of Congress Control Number: 2013932511

Cataloging-in-Publication Data
Strother, Ruth.
 Tarantula / Ruth Strother.
   p. cm. -- (Great Predators)
ISBN 978-1-61783-952-8 (lib. bdg.)
ISBN 978-1-62403-017-8 (pbk.)
Includes bibliographical references and index.
1. Tarantulas--Juvenile literature. 2. Spiders--Juvenile literature. 3. Predatory animals--Juvenile literature.   I. Title.
595.4--dc23
                                             2013932511

Photo Credits: Shutterstock Images, cover, 1, 6; Thinkstock, 4, 10, 18, 20, 23, 26, 45; Biosphoto/SuperStock, 9; Arleen Ng/Tri-Valley Herald/AP Images, 12; Minden Pictures/SuperStock, 14; Ryan M. Bolton/Shutterstock Images, 16, 24; NHPA/SuperStock, 28, 37; Red Line Editorial, 31; FLPA/SuperStock, 33; Jupiterimages/Thinkstock, 34, 43; Nirmalendu Majumdar/Ames Tribune/AP Images, 39; Cathy Keifer/Shutterstock Images, 40

CONTENTS

CHAPTER ONE

MEET THE TARANTULA

A tarantula senses that night is near. It crawls from its silk-lined burrow to the surface. Then it pokes its long, hairy front legs out of the burrow. The spider remains still as the minutes and hours tick by. At last, tiny motion-sensing hairs on the spider's legs begin to vibrate. They are picking up movement nearby. The spider knows another creature

This zebra tarantula may look like a terrifying creature, but these predators are gentler than many people think.

A tarantula devours a beetle larva.

is coming its way. This could be the tarantula's next meal.

A cricket hops by, unaware of the danger. It wanders near the giant spider—too close. The tarantula pounces. It pierces the helpless cricket with its venomous fangs. The paralyzed cricket can do nothing. The tarantula chews open the cricket. Then the spider spits a special juice into its victim.

The juice will liquefy the cricket's insides. Then the tarantula sucks up the fluid as it squeezes the cricket into a ball.

A Scary Spider?

More than 43,000 known spider species exist today. This includes more than 900 tarantula species. Like all spiders, tarantulas are arachnids. All arachnids are spineless and have eight legs. Tarantulas are known for their hairy legs and bodies. These hairs help tarantulas sense the world around them. They can also brush special hairs off their abdomens as a form of defense.

Tarantulas and True Spiders

There are two main categories of spiders. One group includes tarantulas. The other group is known as true spiders. Like all spiders, tarantulas have four pairs of legs, unlike insects, which have three pairs of legs. Tarantulas are different from true spiders because tarantula fangs move in an up-and-down motion. True spiders' fangs move from side to side. The two types of spiders also breathe differently. And the two groups spin different types of webs.

Mistaken Identity

The tarantula got its name from a species of wolf spider. The spider lived in the Italian city of Taranto. Sometime around the 1300s, the people of Taranto believed a wolf spider bite caused a painful and deadly disease called tarantism. Once bitten, the victim often jumped and danced around. The victim's movement was similar to a folk dance called the Tarantella. It turned out that the wolf spider was not really at fault. A different kind of spider caused a tarantism bite. When early Europeans immigrated to America, they saw a large, hairy spider. It looked somewhat like the wolf spider. So they named it tarantula.

Tarantulas live in warm areas around the world. They come in many different colors and sizes. The smallest tarantulas have a leg span of less than one inch (2.5 cm). But the legs of a goliath birdeater tarantula can span a dinner plate. Most tarantulas have legs that span between two and six inches (5–15 cm). Females are usually larger than males.

Many people around the world fear tarantulas. But despite their creepy appearance and eating habits, tarantulas aren't

Goliath birdeater tarantulas are large enough to eat lizards, frogs, and small rodents.

nearly as scary as they seem. Tarantula bites are not known to be deadly to humans. In fact, a honeybee's venom is thought to be stronger than most tarantula venom. Infection and allergic reactions are the biggest concerns from a tarantula bite. Tarantulas are not normally aggressive toward people. These creatures

Because they are not aggressive or dangerous toward humans, tarantulas are popular as pets.

are gentle enough that many people keep them as pets.

Tarantulas may not be dangerous to humans. But they are important predators in their ecosystems.

There are many myths and superstitions surrounding spiders. In *The Adventures of Huckleberry Finn* by Mark Twain, Huck Finn describes an encounter with a spider:

> *Pretty soon a spider went crawling up my shoulder, and I flipped it off and it lit in the candle; and before I could budge it was all shriveled up. I didn't need anybody to tell me that that was an awful bad sign and would fetch me some bad luck, so I was scared and most shook the clothes off of me. I got up and turned around in my tracks three times and crossed my breast every time; and then I tied up a little lock of my hair with a thread to keep witches away. But I hadn't no confidence. . . . I hadn't ever heard anybody say it was any way to keep off bad luck when you'd killed a spider.*

Source: Mark Twain. Adventures of Huckleberry Finn. 1884. Mineola, NY: Dover Publications, 1994. Print. 3.

Changing Minds

This passage talks about Huck Finn's superstitions about spiders. Most of the stories and movies that have been written about spiders, especially tarantulas, cast them in a negative light. What tarantula characteristics might have brought about this point of view? How do those characteristics actually help tarantulas survive? Write a few sentences trying to convince Huck Finn that spiders aren't as frightening as they seem.

CHAPTER TWO

A TARANTULA'S LIFE

Tarantulas are mainly solitary creatures. They prefer to stay near their underground burrows. But males travel beyond their burrows when looking for mates. Males are usually mature and ready to mate when they are about six or seven years old. Females are usually ready when they are between five and ten years old. But mating age varies by species.

Male tarantulas sometimes travel a long way to find a mate, like this tarantula in California.

Female tarantulas often roll their eggs into egg sacs.

Most tarantulas mate in the fall. This is when humans are most likely to see a tarantula.

A male finds a female tarantula by her scent. When he finds a female, he taps on the ground and webbing outside her burrow. If she wants to mate, the female crawls out of her burrow.

Mating

Most female tarantulas produce between 200 and 500 eggs. This takes a lot of energy. Males often run away after mating. The hungry female may try to make the male her next meal. Most males are able to escape the female. But they still die shortly after mating. Male tarantulas will only mate once in their lifetimes.

A female tarantula spins a silk mat in her burrow where she lays her eggs. Some species of tarantula cover these eggs with more silk. Other species wrap the eggs into a ball called an egg sac. The egg sac can be moved around the burrow. The female guards her eggs for six to eight weeks.

Silk

Both male and female tarantulas have spinnerets at the ends of their abdomens. The spinnerets convert a silk protein solution into silk fiber. Tarantulas do not spin sticky spider webs used for capturing food. Instead, they use their silk for a variety of other tasks. They line their burrows with it and use it to protect their eggs.

These baby blue-footed tarantulas look like smaller versions of the adult spiders.

Baby spiders are called spiderlings. Once the spiderlings hatch, they remain in the burrow with their mother for a few days to a few weeks. Then they leave their burrow to begin their solitary lives.

Depending on the species, female tarantulas can live for up to 30 years. The males aren't so lucky. Most male tarantulas don't make it to the age of seven.

Molting

Tarantulas have an outer skeleton called an exoskeleton. The only way a tarantula can grow is by shedding its exoskeleton. This is called molting. Some tarantula species molt once within the egg. Others have their first molt after hatching. Tarantulas molt about four times a year as they are growing. Females molt once a year when mature. Most males don't survive long enough to molt after becoming mature. Male tarantulas that do try to molt usually don't survive.

Before molting, some tarantulas make a mat with their silk. Then the tarantula may lie on its back or remain upright. It pumps up its body to split. This detaches the hard exoskeleton. Molting

The Dangers of Molting

Molting is a dangerous time for a tarantula. A tarantula cannot protect itself from dangers while molting. And a lot can go wrong during the molt. A leg can get stuck. Parts of the exoskeleton can remain attached. If a tarantula loses a leg, it will regrow during the next molt.

Tarantulas' tough exoskeletons do not grow with them, so the spiders must shed their exoskeletons by molting.

can take between 15 minutes and many hours to complete.

After the molt is complete, the new exoskeleton needs to dry and harden. The tarantula can't eat for a few days during this time. Its fangs are too rubbery. But soon the tarantula will be ready for its next meal.

EXPLORE ONLINE

Chapter Two discusses a tarantula's life cycle, including information about molting. The link at the Web site below shows a video of a tarantula molting. As you know, every source is different. How does seeing the tarantula molt help you understand molting better? What information about molting is easier to understand in the text than in the video? What can you learn from the video on this Web site?

Tarantula Molting
www.mycorelibrary.com/tarantula

CHAPTER THREE

MAKING THE KILL

All tarantulas have similar physical characteristics and behaviors. But different species have different versions of these characteristics. All tarantulas are specially equipped for hunting.

Spider Senses

Most tarantulas have eight eyes. This allows them to see in every direction. They may have many eyes, but tarantulas still have poor eyesight. Most tarantulas

Tarantulas are usually ambush hunters. They hide by their burrows and wait for the right time to attack.

Book Lungs

Tarantulas don't breathe the way we do. Instead they have two pairs of book lungs. The book lungs are openings in the abdomen. The openings have thin, stacked flaps arranged much like book pages. Air gets into the book lungs and mixes with fluids within the flaps. Then the fluids circulate the oxygen throughout the tarantula's body.

spend a lot of time underground and hunt at night. They do not need sharp eyesight.

Tarantulas do not have taste buds, ears, or noses. Instead, tarantulas have pedipalps. These are two feelers near a tarantula's face. The pedipalps can move things around. Hollow hairs at the ends of the pedipalps help tarantulas sense whether something is worth eating. It's their way of smelling and tasting.

Tarantulas also have a very strong sense of touch. Specialized hairs on a tarantula's legs can feel vibrations. The tarantula is sure to sense when another creature comes near it. Each of a tarantula's legs also

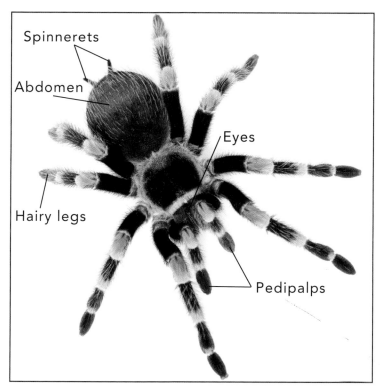

Tarantula
The major parts of a tarantula are shown and labeled in this photo. See if you can write down the function for each body part. Go back and reread the first three chapters to check your work.

has two claws on its tip. These claws grab surfaces.

They help a tarantula catch itself when it falls.

The Kill

With these special senses, tarantulas don't need to

spend much time actively hunting. Instead tarantulas

wait for prey, usually next to their burrows. Tarantulas

Tarantulas use their two fangs to pierce and inject prey with paralyzing venom.

like to eat insects, other spiders, small snakes and lizards, small rodents, and even small birds. When they sense prey nearby, the tarantulas pounce. They grab the prey with their pedipalps and pierce it with their hollow, venomous fangs.

The moment a tarantula sinks its fangs into its prey, the venom goes to work. Almost immediately the prey cannot move. Tarantulas often drag their prey into their burrows after paralyzing it. Now the tarantula can enjoy its meal.

Tarantulas are not able to eat solid food. They need to turn their prey into liquid. A tarantula's mouthparts have thin hairs and tiny teeth-like spikes. Tarantulas use these spikes to tear open prey and expose its soft insides. The tarantula spits up digestive juices onto the prey to liquefy its innards. Muscles surround a tarantula's stomach. The muscles squeeze the stomach in pulses. This creates a pumping action.

Thirsty Spiders

Tarantulas need to stay hydrated to be at the top of their game. Tarantulas use muscles to bend their seven-segmented legs before pouncing. They need to pump blood into their legs to extend them. If a tarantula hasn't had enough water, it won't be able to pump enough blood for the legs to extend. This definitely affects its pouncing success.

A tarantula eats a cicada in the Amazon.

The pumping helps draw prey juices through the tarantula's straw-like mouth into its stomach.

The tarantula's pedipalps hold the prey while the spider slurps up its meal. The pedipalps squeeze the prey as the tarantula sucks away its juices. By the time the meal is done, the spider has rolled whatever is left of the prey into a ball called a bolus. The bolus is discarded.

Scientists once thought tarantulas shot silk from their feet. The passage below is from a study with a different conclusion. These scientists claim that sense organs are all that can be found on tarantulas' feet, proving the silk-shooting theory wrong:

> Two studies have claimed that 'ribbed hairs' on the tarsi of tarantulas produce silk. . . . We found that, morphologically, these ribbed hairs correspond very closely to known chemosensitive hairs in spiders; they have a distinct socket, a bent hair shaft with fine cuticular ridges, an eccentric double lumen within the hair shaft, and a blunt tip with a subterminal pore. Spigots on the spinnerets have a large bulbous base instead of a socket, a long shaft with a scaly surface and a central terminal pore. We never observed any silk threads coming out of these ribbed hairs under the electron microscope.

> Source: Rainer F. Foelix et al. "Silk Secretion from Tarantula Feet Revisited: Alleged Spigots Are Probably Chemoreceptors." The Journal of Experimental Biology. The Company of Biologists, 2012. Web. Accessed December 2, 2012.

Back It Up

The scientists of this study use evidence to support their point that tarantulas don't shoot silk from their feet. Write a paragraph describing what the scientists have proven. Then write down the evidence these scientists use to back up their findings.

CHAPTER FOUR

HABITAT AND RANGE

Tarantulas can be found all over the world. They can survive in both dry and tropical climates as long as the weather is warm much of the year. Tarantulas that live in dry climates make their homes in desert or semi-desert regions. They usually live in underground burrows. Tarantulas that live in tropical climates live in forests. They live on the ground or in the trees. In the United States, tarantulas can

This pink-toed tarantula of Trinidad lives in a nest in a tree.

Two Worlds of Tarantulas

Tarantulas are often classified as being either New World or Old World tarantulas. The New World includes regions in the Western Hemisphere, such as North, Central, and South America. The Old World includes regions in the Eastern Hemisphere, such as Africa, Asia, and India. The Old World tarantulas tend to have a more slender, longer abdomen. They also tend to be more aggressive than their New World relatives.

be found west of the Mississippi River. They live as far north as central California, Utah, and Missouri

Tarantulas in the Trees

Tree-dwelling tarantulas are known as arboreal tarantulas. Arboreal tarantulas tend to be smaller, lighter in weight, and more colorful than those that live underground. They also have longer, thinner abdomens. Arboreal tarantulas are usually quicker and more aggressive than the ground-dwelling spiders. They also have wider pads with more hairs on the ends of their feet. This helps them walk up and down trees more securely.

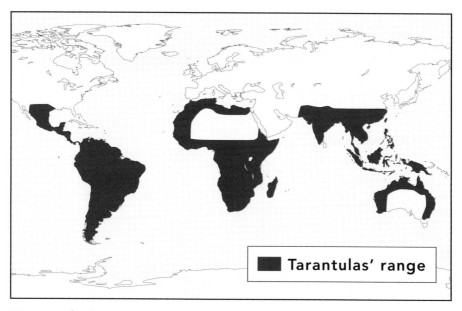

Tarantulas' range

Tarantula Range Map

This map shows the range of tarantulas. Most tarantulas live in the southern countries. Can you tell where the New World and Old World countries are? Reread this chapter and list the differences between the Old World and New World tarantulas. What are their similarities and differences?

Some arboreal tarantulas live in little pouches they make out of silk. The pouch is attached to a branch or other structure. Other arboreal tarantulas make their homes under loose bark or holes in trees. They use their silk to line the area and cover the hole. This helps keep the arboreal tarantulas' homes at the proper temperature and humidity level.

Swimming Spiders

Arboreal tarantulas have been known to flee from enemies by jumping out of trees. Sometimes they land in water. The larger footpads help them swim. The hairs on their feet trap air and help keep them from sinking. However, tarantulas don't jump much because they are fragile. Even a tumble of just a couple of inches could harm a tarantula.

Underground Tarantulas

Tarantulas that live in the ground are known as terrestrial tarantulas. Some terrestrial tarantulas don't bother digging a permanent home. Instead they may find shelter under rocks or fallen branches. But most of these spiders dig burrows for their homes.

A terrestrial tarantula probably digs its burrow as a spiderling, shortly after leaving its birth burrow. Tarantulas use their mouthparts and pedipalps to dig the burrow. Most tarantula burrows are one to two feet (0.3–0.6 m) long. The spider extends its burrow deeper as it grows older.

Most tarantulas live in burrows they dig in the earth.

Tarantulas line their burrows with silk. Tarantulas sometimes cover the burrow opening with silk during the day. This keeps out insects and hides the burrow from potential predators. The silk also helps control temperature and humidity levels inside the burrow.

In the colder months of winter, tarantulas plug the entrance to their burrows with a mixture of silk and soil. They spend the winter resting. In the spring, they remove the plug and warm themselves up. Then it is time to start catching prey.

PREDATORS AND OTHER THREATS

Tarantulas are excellent predators. But even these crafty hunters have predators of their own. Owls, skunks, snakes, lizards, and birds think tarantulas are tasty. But a tarantula's most dangerous predator is a nectar-drinking insect.

The Tarantula Hawk Wasp

The adult tarantula hawk wasp doesn't eat tarantulas. This two-inch-long (5-cm-long) wasp feeds peacefully

When a tarantula is threatened by a predator, it often raises its front legs and pedipalps to seem bigger and scarier.

Tarantula Defenses

When a tarantula is threatened, it often tries to dart into its burrow. But tarantulas have other methods of defense. Some tarantulas will bite when threatened. Others will use special postures to make them appear larger and more dangerous. Many New World tarantulas brush out special hairs onto their attackers. These are known as urticating hairs. The hairs sting and itch when lodged in a predator's skin or eyes. The barbs make the hairs difficult to remove. Urticating hairs are good repellants. Some tarantula species even weave them into their egg sacs and molting mats for extra protection.

on nectar. But when egg-laying time draws near, the tarantula hawk wasp uses the spiders to provide for its young.

The female wasp uses its sense of smell to search for a tarantula. Then it stings the tarantula, injecting the spider with paralyzing venom. Next the wasp drags the still-living tarantula into the spider's burrow. The wasp lays one egg on the tarantula. After the larva, called a grub, hatches, it spends its first month slowly eating the tarantula alive.

A tarantula hawk wasp bites the legs off a tarantula.

It eventually eats the tarantula's organs, killing the tarantula. Then the wasp emerges from the burrow as an adult.

Other Dangers

Tarantula hawk wasps are some of tarantulas' fiercest predators. But the biggest threat to tarantulas is the loss of their habitat. As the human population spreads out, people move into the spiders' territory. Wildlife areas get leveled to build cities. Logging and other

Snacking on Spiders

People eat tarantulas in some parts of the world. People in Cambodia began eating tarantulas in great numbers in the 1970s. During that time there were food restrictions that drove people to turn to the spiders as a food source. These tarantulas are fried in garlic and salt and often sold by the sides of roads. In Venezuela, tarantulas are wrapped in leaves, seasoned, and roasted over a fire. The fangs are used as toothpicks.

practices kill off parts of rain forests and many of the animals that live there, including tarantulas.

The souvenir trade is another threat to tarantula populations. Tarantulas are killed and mounted. Then the mounted spiders are sold to tourists. Tarantulas are also popular pets. Many pet tarantulas are captured from the wild. This practice further threatens populations of tarantulas in the wild. Many tarantula species are bred in captivity. This allows people to have pet tarantulas without harming the wild population. Tarantula enthusiasts encourage

Tarantulas bred in captivity make great pets without threatening wild tarantula populations.

captive breeding because it helps protect some threatened species from becoming extinct.

Why We Need Tarantulas

It's important to protect tarantulas. They are predators that help control insect populations. Scientists are also finding medicinal uses for tarantulas. For example, chemicals in the Chilean rose tarantula may help cure

The green blue bottle tarantula is one of the most colorful species of tarantula.

FURTHER EVIDENCE

A variety of threats to tarantulas are discussed in Chapter Five. Some threats come from predators. Others come from humans. What is the main point of the chapter? What evidence is given to support that point? Visit the Web site at the link below. Find a quote from the Web site that supports the chapter's main point. Does the quote support existing evidence in the chapter? Or does it add a new piece of evidence?

Tarantulas and Deforestation

www.mycorelibrary.com/tarantula

muscular dystrophy. The effects of these chemicals on arthritis and certain cancers are also being studied.

Tarantulas are one of the most misunderstood predators around. Many people are frightened of the spiders. But tarantulas are an important part of their ecosystems. Learning more about these amazing predators and how to protect them will help make sure these amazing hunters stick around.

Common Name: Tarantula

Scientific Name: *Theraphosidae*

Average Size: Leg span between two and six inches (5–15 cm)

Average Weight: One to three ounces (28–100 g)

Color: Usually brown or black, but can vary depending on species; some are brightly colored

Average Lifespan: Males usually live fewer than seven years, depending on the species; females live up to 30 years, depending on the species

Diet: Insects, other spiders, small snakes and lizards, small rodents, and small birds

Habitat: Warm regions around the world, including deserts and rainforests

Predators: Owls, skunks, snakes, lizards, birds, tarantula hawk wasps, and humans

Did You Know?

- Tarantulas can go weeks without eating.
- A tarantula's blood looks blue.
- Some older tarantulas have a bald spot on their back ends.

Why Do I Care?

Chapter Five discusses some of the threats faced by tarantulas. Habitat loss and the pet trade are two of the biggest threats to tarantula populations. Why is it important to protect tarantulas from those threats? How does the existence of tarantulas affect your life?

Dig Deeper

Now that you've read this book, what questions do you still have about tarantulas? Write down one or two questions that can guide you in doing research. With an adult's help, find a few reliable sources about tarantulas or spiders in general that can help answer your questions. Write a few sentences about how you did your research and what you learned from it.

Say What?

This book gives you a glimpse into the world of tarantulas. Find five words in this book that you've never heard before. Use a dictionary to find out what they mean. Then write the meanings in your own words, and use each word in a new sentence.

Tell the Tale

Pretend you're a tarantula. Write 200 words describing a night in the life of a tarantula. What is it like to emerge from a burrow? Wait for prey? Rely on vibrations for most of your information? How does it feel to molt? Be sure to set the scene, develop a sequence of events, and offer a conclusion.

GLOSSARY

arboreal
living in trees

bolus
a round mass of chewed food

burrow
an underground home made by an animal and used for shelter

ecosystem
the group of plants and animals living in and interacting with their environment

exoskeleton
the hard case covering a tarantula

extinct
a species that has completely died out

paralyze
to make an animal unable to move

pedipalps
two appendages near the mouth of a tarantula that look like short legs

species
a group of similar animals that are closely related enough to mate with one another

spinnerets
two fingerlike structures on the rear of a tarantula that spin silk

venom
toxic liquid injected into prey or enemies by biting or stinging

LEARN MORE

Books

Britton, Tamara L. *Tarantula Spiders.* Edina, MN: ABDO, 2011.

Franchino, Vicky. *Tarantula.* New York: Scholastic, 2012.

Montgomery, Sy. *The Tarantula Scientist.* Boston: Houghton Mifflin, 2004.

Web Links

To learn more about tarantulas, visit ABDO Publishing Company online at **www.abdopublishing.com**. Web sites about tarantulas are featured on our Book Links page. These links are routinely monitored and updated to provide the most current information available.

Visit **www.mycorelibrary.com** for free additional tools for teachers and students.

INDEX

ABOUT THE AUTHOR

Ruth Strother has written and edited numerous award-winning books for children and adults. She was born in New York, grew up in Minnesota, and is now trying to warm up in Southern California.